AF413811

NATURE'S GRACE

NATURE'S GRACE

DIANA HOWARD

atmosphere press

© 2024 Diana Howard

Published by Atmosphere Press

Cover design by Ronaldo Alves

No part of this book may be reproduced without permission from the author except in brief quotations and in reviews.

Atmospherepress.com

A curious, contemplative birch tree
lives outside my kitchen window.
It houses robins in the spring,
their nest cuddled in a crevice of two branches.
Its leaves droop like a willow,
sway like feathers in the morning breeze.

Table of Contents

DAY

Sunlight trickles through drawn shade as muscles yearn to move.
Leaves unfold, blossoms spread, deer roam fields of bluestem.
Sparrows gather at the bird bath. Seconds turn into minutes,
turn into hours as we move, commune, accomplish.
We raise our shade to the calling of a dove each day.

Morning Walk

baby opossum

    perfectly formed

      let go too soon

back to mother earth

  enriches

    anemones

  coneflowers

    yellow clover

  where

    honey bees

  land

    sucking

clear

  sweet

    nectar

beside

 river

  river

  river

monarchs

 embrace

rosy milkweed

twee

 twee

  too – wee

sings oriole.

Morning Meditation

There is a hint of pink in the eastern sky,
a sliver of fuchsia gradually widening

its embrace of the morning sun.
I've brought in a pile of wood.

Made a simple fire. There aren't many
wood burners anymore,

no patience for soot or sparks or the carrying
in of anything that might be heavy or messy.

Outside my window, Canada geese
begin to stir with the day's first light,

taking wing in perfect symmetry.
My fire, now a rich smoldering

to ash, has left me remembering
there is more wood out back.

Perpetuity

Forest trees have evolved to live in cooperative, interdependent relationships, maintained by communication and a collective intelligence not unlike an insect colony. These soaring columns of living wood draw the eye upward to their outspreading crowns, but the real action is taking place underground, just a few inches below our feet.

—*Richard Grant*

Out of dying bramble,
fallen limbs and
rotted stumps
does a spirit rise?

Does a fledgling cottonwood
look to its mother,
follow in her footsteps,
see her spirit rise in death?

My mother loved the woods.
She was drawn to its quiet mystery,
its blossoming leaves of spring,
radiant colors of fall.

She grew up strong
with arms that protected,
nourished, embraced,
her thoughts revealed in song.

As I watched her take
her last breath, her chest
depleted of air, I saw a
faint shadow rise

like the tree.

On Sabbatical

I woke to find you
wandering around
in my head
with a searchlight.

I wanted to tell you
not to worry
that I am not lost,
nor am I wishing at this

moment to be found, yet
I do hear you earnestly
calling my name.
Since you are only a thought

I am not sure how to respond.
Even with all the justifiable
clever retorts that live in my head,
I find myself dipping low

to the ground to avoid detection.
I find a quiet place,
just off the trail where musty scents
of dew and lichen wrap around me like cashmere,

a place where I can whisper
what I know to be true
and watch the trees
nod in agreement.

Wild Mustard

shadows the Missouri River shoreline—
a quarter acre filled with golden flowered stalks,
something Van Gogh would have painted—
something Frost would have embraced
with his marvelous words. They knew what our earth
offers, what was, and still is, here for a reason.
Such a simple treasure, ignored by most.
As days go by, the quarter acre will succumb
to the urge of a contractor's excavation.
I will rescue some before that happens —
hold on to another strong yet gentle gift
from this holy field.

Things to See in the Woods

Deer trails
The first bloodwort of spring
The last snakeroot of fall
Another morel mushroom
A fox peeking out of its hole
Three leaves to leave be
Magnolia blossoms floating in the breeze
A fawn curled around itself, waiting.

Walking with Mary Oliver

We are kindred
with the wild inside us,

a mournful howl
we both know well,

how our eyes keenly
search the dark,

vigilant to a fault.
We are kindred

with the wild inside us
in our fierce longing

to protect and defend.
Alpha drives

Omega softens.
We are kindred

in our hunting beneath dead
leaves and rotted limbs,

baring the forest floor
in search of our roots.

One Poet's Heart

In honor of Wendell Berry

She watched him through the trees,
bag in hand, gathering empty beer cans.
His shoulders slumped, he reaches
down. Doing my part, he says.
We need a cart, she says, to hold them all.
He is at home in these woods.
The only thing a coyote leaves behind
is scat or a rabbit bone, he murmurs.
Things the earth can swallow
without choking. There is wisdom
in the wild, he says. The coyote knows
as does the rabbit, the badger, the buck.
He knows he must do more than write about it,
curled up in his office, words flowing
from his fingers. How could that possibly
be enough?

Deerspeak

If I had not looked up when I did,
I would have missed you
standing just to the right
of the crushed limestone path,
statuesque, purposeful,
your cautious stare
framed by the delicacy
of a spring dogwood branch.

I half-expected you to speak
about the way my footsteps
navigated through the brush,
inept and stumbling.

I expected wisdom.
I hoped for grace.

I imagined following you
on the trail you had made,
leaping over fallen trees,
blithely skipping
through grassy fields.

I remain most grateful
for the way you spoke to me that day,
your eyes never leaving mine,

telling me to press on unafraid.

Into the Woods

I went to the woods
following a loon's haunting call.

She floated on the edge of wildness
where pristine lake water lapped

against brown cattails and pink yarrow;
where Canada pine gathered

tall and thick along the shoreline like
sentries holding down a fort.

She led me into the woods,
left me sitting on a blade-cut

cedar pine stump, surrounded
by a quiet just beginning to waken.

I heard the sound of a tender
dewdrop meeting a sinewy fern.

I heard my whispers echo
through caverns of sheltering

oak and fir, only to have them
flung back at me like buckshot.

I cried out to the loon from deep
in the forest, she answered back.

Call of the Wild

A falconer strives for relationship
of eye to sharp eye – a voice that commands.
His hawk, a raptor with a talon grip
waits, impatient – its leg chained to a stand.

A falconer's faith, though fearful at best,
sends the hawk soaring in search of its prey.
The hawk follows its heart, its flight a test
of the teacher's trust that it knows the way.

The hawk leaves its master cautious and cold,
wavering in trust of hawk's loyalty.
But what of the hawk whose killing is bold,
whose flight lingers with a wild hope to flee?

What does it owe to the one who pulls taught
when it's hawk's freedom to be that is sought?

The Innate Wisdom of Birds

Let the Birds of the Earth speak to you.   *—Job 12:7-10*

Imagine their language,
  observe their movements,

their way of praying. See how
  the wind folds their wings

and bows their heads.
  See how fearless they are.

They are taught by family
  and peers.

They are watched from above
  as they stumble along

quick to learn what will
  make them strong.

I watch a wren fly
  to my birdhouse,

a foot long stick horizontal
  in its beak. It perches,

pushes once, flies away.
  Moments later

It returns with the stick
  again in its beak.

Now vertical,
  it slides quickly

into the birdhouse.
  It flies away and returns,

again and again
  this amazing wren.

There was no guessing,
  no coincidence

no luck involved,
  just perseverance,

knowledge
  and creativity.

With a brain
  the size of a dime

It's a miracle
  every time.

Black-Browed Babbler

I feel a kinship with the Black-Browed Babbler. I haven't been hid-
ing for 170 years, with most trained ornithologists thinking I'm
extinct, though I do love a good hiding place. Where it has been
and why it has decided to make itself seen and heard is now under
investigation in Borneo off the coast of Indonesia. As a child, I
learned to watch for birds and listen for their calls. As an adult I
carry with me a profound respect for their wisdom and tenacity.

I was curious, one morning, as a red-tailed hawk followed me
along a trail, just over my right shoulder. I was fascinated one
afternoon while writing, to see a pair of goldfinches perched on
my patio door, peering inside, pecking at the window. They ended
up in the poem I was working on. Many times I have thought
to myself, I wish human beings could appreciate their strength,
endurance and cleverness. I do not take birds for granted nor
would I ever shoot them for pleasure. They inspire me, teach me
and give me hope. So why such a kinship
with the Black-Browed Babbler, you ask? I love words, can babble
on for hours AND
my eyebrows-well they used to be black.

The Pelicans

You will wonder, the first time
you see them appear high above you,

their expansive white wings tipped
in black, what kind of birds

dance in the sky like drunken butterflies
swooping and bending in a magnificent waltz?

My first time, I stood transfixed,
in awe of their grace, humming

Strauss under my breath, when
I remembered to breathe,

for the raw beauty of their presence
made me weep.

"Dance, they whispered—and the
world that matters will dance with you."

Sand Hill Crane Migration

It begins with a "V" of three
hovering like drones
above a reedy roadside marsh,
red crests glistening,
gracefully awkward in flight.

A cold sun dawns as steam
rises from placid currents.
Raucous chatter echoes
throughout a once vacant
Nebraska river valley.

A riotous rush of flapping wings,
thousands strong, turns
a morning sun black.
Witness an ancient, driving
homophony that feeds one's soul.

Swallow-tailed Kite

It winged over me,
eyes fixed, as if it knew
my path or what ancient
part of me would hold
the message that had sprung
from its eyes to mine.
I was reminded to do
what would bring me peace.
Though weighted, I longed to fly
when the wind curled around me.
Circling, the Kite returned with
a fervent call to honor its
message. No longer caught,
I released my clenched fists
stretching upward with
the knowledge that I will
claim soaring flight,
the very heart of this bird,
for my own.

Death of a Goldfinch

My hand is open
Holding nothing then
Holding something
Gently weighted
Feather soft
Eyes closed
Yellow-gray
Feet curled
Heart stopped
My hand is open
Then closed
Holding nothing

Mariposa Lily

(for Julie, Barb, and Teri)

A Mariposa lily bulb
holds a tapered stem with white petals

that gently unfold at day's first light.
We spotted one, standing alone

among clusters of lavender bee balm and white yarrow
as we walked The Mickelson Trail.

Before the crushed limestone trail, before the highway
there was only a rough path laid out along a stream

by the hooves of white-tailed deer; a weathered foot trail
for Lakota women foraging a treasured lily bulb.

As the trail opened,
we learned about the landscape,

we learned about each other. We took
shelter in that mountain meadow cabin.

Remember the moment when
thunderheads rolled dropping

handfuls of two inch hail,
how a glowing orange full moon

teased us by simmering behind the edges of the
fading storm clouds, only to majestically appear seconds later?

We were reminded in those Black Hills
that sacredness can be found

in voices that rise from the ground,
and in words that are spoken from our hearts,

words about family and life,
truths about hardship and loss.

A Mariposa Lily has but one blossom
light and winged as its namesake, the butterfly,

yet along the trail it joins a chorus
of color, depth and harmony.

Pacific Coast Highway

I stand on a cliff above an ancient shoreline.
There is no one below exploring the inside
of a conch shell or trudging willingly through
sandy crevasses with grains caressing their toes,
no one brushing aside piles of tender kelp.

It is rare to find a beach void of human footprints.
Rare for mine to be the first of the day.
Plovers scurry to and from, skirting hungry sand crabs.
Seagulls walk alongside hoping for a bite.
They listen to me count my blessings.

The Rescue of a Cabbage Butterfly

It was perched on the edge
of my window sill
quiet and still.

It never occurred to me
that it was inside not outside,
until the next morning

when it was still there
glued to the wood frame,
its wings compressed,

a pale yellow triangle.
I saw an eye that didn't blink,
a heart that didn't pulse

until I gently touched it.
Will it let me help it flee?
I pinched its wings together,

carried it fluttering
to my patio door. What joy
it expressed as I set it free

to dance in the sunlight.
What joy I felt at the life
 I had saved.

Its eyes, I learned, were filled with
thousands of lenses that view
our shared world as a complex mosaic.

How I wish I could have seen my world
through its eyes that never close,
this 2-inch, paper thin, winged miracle.

51

The Way of a Turtle

There is the determined
way a loggerhead turtle finds,
to return to what she knows.

She goes back to where
she began and begins again.
As buoyant currents

bend, shape, and teach,
she journeys across the floor
of a vast ocean,

thousands of miles.

She feels no pride in her
progress nor frustration
with her obstacles.

She knows when to move.
She knows when to rest.
As her journey ends,

another life begins.

Cape Horn

Packing a wounded heart,
I went to the end of the earth,
a Chilean Archipelago
that spoke of
predator and prey
lichen and layers
granite and glacier
repetition and recession
indigenous and independence
confluence and courage
sand, silk, clay,
turbidite and oblate spheroid.

I learned not to avoid
impoverished landscapes
for appearances can be deceiving.
Truth will wind its way through
crevasses, bubbling up over
gathering sediment.
Packing a wounded heart
I went to the end of the earth.
Unsheathed...
I inhaled its glory.

Winter

Brutal, bitter cold,
a biting wind howls.
I long for the sunlit
songs of summer.

Sub zero, hard
to breathe, my
mask muffles
my words, I need

the tender songs
of summer. I seek
a warm fire,
a hot cup of tea.

Bitter cold
the eagle cries,
the ganders raise
their wings to fly.

They search for
the fervent songs
of summer.

Firestorm

Virulent, sweeping balls
of red-orange flame
abruptly scatter those
who live in tandem with it.

A firestorm doesn't ask permission.

A careless spark, randomly tossed,
can change a landscape
and those who embrace it
forever.

A firestorm engulfs the weak.

Even the strongest are
brought to their knees as it
showers the ground
with smoldering ash.

A firestorm respects no boundaries.

I have seen land
stripped bare for miles,
a lone blade of grass,
brilliant green

giving hope to a ravaged land.

Missouri River

*There is only one river with a personality, a sense of humor and a woman's caprice; a
river that goes traveling sideways, a river that plays hide and seek with you today and
tomorrow follows you around like a pet dog with a dynamite cracker tied to his tail.
That river is the Missouri.*   —George Fitch

It travels east then south,
    a gentle swirling that is
        more dangerous than it appears,
           its banks, steep and rocky.

        Some years, there is
      so little rain that one
    could almost wade to
the other side.

Some years, the banks disappear as flood waters inundate, altering
    its shape and size.

The river flows across the street
    from my house. It is quiet,
      gentle and wandering,
        never tiring of its path.

      Never tiring of eagles
     that feed off carp and catfish,
  never weary of nature's gathering
of hoary verbena, prairie sage and willows,

bluestem and switchgrass;
    sunflowers that gather for miles in the fall.

Geese
      that
         float
            downstream.

The river wasn't always
    this narrow or this deep.
        Migration west in the 1800's
            challenged pioneers

        to wade through miles
      of shallow waters, sometimes
    laden with prairie grass,
sometimes thick with mud.

        As their settlements grew,
      river land became farmland.
    In 1927, flood control measures
were taken with caution and hope.

The river flows today, with determination,
    but its spirit is dampened,
        its natural habitat endangered,
            its reservoirs filling with sediment.

        What will always remain is a legacy
      going back millions of years,
    a fortress of water answering its call
while giving its heart in return.

A Moonbeam Deified

Like a shimmering tendril reaching
down from a black pearl sky,
a moonbeam wound its way through
layers of asteroids and atmospheric gasses,
through earthly shields of cloud and smog,
penetrating with divine intensity,
gangly cottonwood branches.

What touched me
was the energy it still had
after a long night of rescuing
aimlessly wandering stars, to settle
against the quiet folds of my bed.

NIGHT

darkening the rim of day, one's breath, measured by the hoot of an owl,
the stealth of a deer's hoof, the call of a whip – poor – will.
Night, walking in shoes of the blind, learning to trust scent and touch.
Night holding watch over fears and dreams, taking solace
from an ever-present moon.

Author's notes

A special thank you to my brother Mike,
my dear writing friend Nan
and my Poetry Group
for their patience and excellent
feedback as I shared these poems with them.

I was raised with the teaching that nature
with all its gifts
is to be respected, cared for and
appreciated. It gives me more than
I can ever repay.

Diana Howard, 2023

About Atmosphere Press

Founded in 2015, Atmosphere Press was built on the principles of Honesty, Transparency, Professionalism, Kindness, and Making Your Book Awesome. As an ethical and author-friendly hybrid press, we stay true to that founding mission today.

If you're a reader, enter our giveaway for a free book here:

SCAN TO ENTER
BOOK GIVEAWAY

If you're a writer, submit your manuscript for consideration here:

SCAN TO SUBMIT
MANUSCRIPT

And always feel free to visit Atmosphere Press and our authors online at atmospherepress.com. See you there soon!

About the Author

DIANA HOWARD is a poet and children's author who lives beside the Missouri River. *Nature's Grace* is her second chapbook and one in which she takes special pride. It speaks to her heart and her faith.

Diana began writing poetry in earnest when she was thirty-seven. Now at age seventy-three, she is amazed at what she has produced over the years. She is grateful to have found Atmosphere Press – people who are kind, qualified, and easy to work with.

Over the years, she has been told that she has a way with words. Today she has deep appreciation for her life's journey.

www.ingramcontent.com/pod-product-compliance
Lightning Source LLC
Chambersburg PA
CBHW022047150726
48196CB00074B/787/J